The Late Medieval Fabric

The 120ft spire of All Saints was completed in the early 15th century

The church took on its present form in the late 14th century when the tower and spire were erected, the nave extended and the arcades reconstructed. It is possible that almost the whole of the old church was demolished, leaving only the easternmost bays standing in order that mass might continue at the altars. The tower, octagon and 120 foot spire were the first part of the new work to be constructed, this was underway in 1394 when Richard Byrd gave money in his will to the new fabric. The rest of the building must have been all but complete by about 1410 when work began on glazing the north and south walls (see below). The modest way the arcades were rebuilt, using old material and with minimum detail, suggests that by the 15th century, after the extravagance of the tower and spire, the amount of money available for the work was restricted. In the 1440s the roof was still not complete and although bequests of tiles and lead were made in order that work might proceed 'within a few years' the work was only completed in the 1470s when the lavish ceilings over the chancel ⌐ installed.

Altars, chantries and ornaments

cross light before the rood and a light at the Easter Sepulchre on the north side of the chancel.

There may have been as many as eight chantries established at the altars to say mass for the souls of deceased benefactors of the church. We have details of only a few. The earliest was founded in 1324 by John Benge at the altar of our Lady. Two more were founded in 1410, one by William Vescy at the altar of St Thomas the Martyr, and the second by Adam del Bank and John Bawtrie at the altar of St Nicholas. In the early 16th century a number of chantries (including that of the Bolton family at the altar of our Lady) were amalgamated. Each altar and chantry was individually endowed with all the plate and vestments necessary for a priest to sing mass. William Vescy gave to his chantry two silver vessels to make a chalice and a length of linen cloth to

By the end of the Middle Ages in addition to the 'high' altar in the chancel, there were at least four and possibly five other altars in the church. We know that one was dedicated to the Blessed Virgin Mary and was situated in the north 'Lady choir,' where a statue of her was also kept. The altar of St Nicholas was situated in the south choir aisle known as the 'choir of St Nicholas and St Katherine', and two further altars of St Thomas the Martyr and St James the Great, stood in the north and south nave aisles. In addition to these altars there were also a number of lights burning before images. In the early 15th century there was a light before 'our Lady', a 'St Crux' or holy

ABOVE: John Bawtrie, a member of the Minster clergy, founded a chantry in the church in 1410.

RIGHT: All Saints Cottages next to the church were probably built in the 15th century to support a chantry.

Emma Raughton and Our Lady of North Street

At the west end of the south aisle you will see inset into the wall an opening called a squint. This originally enabled a hermit, or anchorite, who occupied an 'anchorhold', a two-storey house attached to the aisle, a view of the altars in the church. In the 1420s and 30s a visionary named Emma Raughton was living here. We would know nothing of Emma, if she had not received a series of visions of the Blessed Virgin Mary, which were of political significance. They were recorded in the *Beauchamp Pageant* and the *Rous Roll,* annals of the life of Richard Beauchamp, Earl of Warwick. Emma received our Lady seven times in 1421, who informed her of the impending death of Henry V and the coronation of Henry VI as king of France. Through our Lady's revelation Emma was able to tell Richard Beauchamp, who visited her from time to time, that he would serve as Protector of the young king until he came of age. Emma's anchorhold was demolished when it ceased to be used, probably at the Reformation. In 1910, the churchwarden Edwin Ridsdale Tate constructed the present anchorhold of timber and shuttered concrete on the site of the medieval building. A number of 'anchorites' have occupied it this century, the last and the most memorable being 'Brother' Walter Wilman, who lived in it from the 1930s to 60s.

LEFT: Ridsdale Tate's anchorhold is built on the site of Emma Raughton's house.

ABOVE: St Ann teaching the Virgin Mary to read – glass in the Blackburn window.

make albs, amices and other vestments. These basics were constantly being augmented through bequests. In the 1455 will of Sir John Cliff, chaplain of Benge's chantry, he gave to his altar 'a red vestment of cloth of gold', and to the altar of St James 'a grey vestment with black orphreys (strips of embroidery) worked with gold, another with red orphreys worked with garters, and all his altar apparel'.

The chantries provided All Saints with a clerical staff as large as some of the great collegiate churches. In the early 15th century there were at least three chantry priests, who along with the rector and his assistant the parochial chaplain, ensured that there was a constant supply of masses throughout the day.

The Medieval stained glass

The medieval stained glass in All Saints is internationally famous. In few churches can you see so great, or so varied a display. The glazing dates from two phases, coinciding with rebuilding campaigns. The earliest glass is from the first half of the 14th century when the east-end was rebuilt, and the rest, the majority, is from the 15th century, when among other work, the north and south walls were rebuilt.

The 14th century glass is confined to the east windows of the north and south aisles. Originally that in the north aisle occupied the window behind the high altar. Reflecting the fashion of the period, the imagery in these windows is elegantly spaced in bands or rows, each under a canopy that reflects the prevailing architectural style of the time, with expansive backgrounds of trailing foliage, and borders of foliage, covered cups or castles. Each window has a central dominating

The Annunciation – part of the Joys of the Virgin window of c1340.

RIGHT: *Detail from the Corporal Acts of Mercy window – visiting the sick.*

4

Crucifix, which was intended to function as the cross for the altar below.

Nine windows contain glass from the second phase of glazing, which took some time to finance and install, the campaign commencing around 1410 when the *Pricke of Conscience* window was put in and continuing throughout the 1420s and 30s. The Orders of Angels window in the south aisle was probably among the last to be installed.

The cost of the glazing fell upon the richer inhabitants of the parish, who often worked together as family groups or collaborated with friends and neighbours to buy a window. The donors were keen to immortalise themselves and their generosity, so we see the kneeling images of the Bawtrie, Henryson, Hessle, Blackburn and Baguley families at the bottom of the windows. Some of the figures of standing saints in the glass were the result of their personal religious interests. The imagery in the Blackburn window, with its dominating figure of St Ann, was influenced by Nicholas Blackburn's fondness for that saint. In some cases the imagery reflected the window's location within the church, for example the images of St Thomas the Apostle and St Thomas of Canterbury stood over the altar of St Thomas the Martyr in the north aisle.

Three of the windows consist of a series of panels that were intended instruct the viewer. The imagery and texts within the Corporal Acts of Mercy, the Order of Angels and the Pricke of Conscience windows reinforce ideas of medieval social conscience, hierarchy and repentance.

All the medieval stained glass has been restored at some point in its history. Wailes of Newcastle undertook major work in 1844 and further 'restoration' and re-arrangement was done in the 1860s and 1960s.

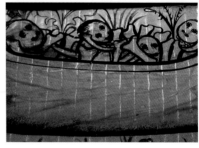

ABOVE: *Dead men's bones rise – the 12th day according to the Pricke of Conscience.*

TOP: *A detail from the Orders of Angels window.*

5

fabric continued as before. In 1695 John Etty constructed a new altar-piece and Mr Graime was paid for 'painting a dove' [the Holy Ghost?] on it.

With the medieval altars went the large staff of priests that served them. By the end of the 16th century All Saints was served by a basic provision of rector and lay parish clerk. The living was always poorly endowed, and as early as 1548 there was a plan to amalgamate the parish with that of St John Ousegate and to demolish All Saints.

The maintenance of the church fabric and the poor of the parish were supported by charities that generated income from local properties. Some of these properties, including the 15th century row called All Saints cottages, which face the north wall of the church, had probably supported chantries before the Reformation. The income from property was augmented through bequests: Ann Orfeur in 1790 and Dorothy Bowes in 1794 left £100 each to be invested to provide coals for the poor.

After the Reformation – c1550-1900

The Reformation had an immense impact on All Saints. The multiple altars and their ornamentation were gradually swept away under the reforming legislation of Edward VI and Elizabeth I. The interior was altered beyond recognition, the open spaces in the aisles and choirs being filled with box-pews and the high altar replaced by a railed communion table. The focus of the church shifted from sacrament to word, and from 1675 the present pulpit, part of a double-decker, dominated the interior. The work of maintaining and beautifying the

TOP: The box-pewed interior of All Saints prior to the 19th century restoration.

LEFT: The chancel of All Saints in the early years of Patrick Shaw's incumbency.

6

Anglo-Catholic Revival

From the 1860s under George Guest and subsequent rectors, All Saints was already moving in an Anglo-Catholic direction, but it was not until 1904 when a young priest called Patrick Shaw was instituted to the rectory that the church was firmly established in this tradition. Shaw had arrived in York in the 1890s and served his title at St Olave's, a church at the cutting-edge of the Anglo-Catholic revival in the city. In the 1890s St Olave's had adopted for its celebration of communion the ceremonial of the 'English Use' based on the precedent of the medieval 'Sarum' or Salisbury rite. When Shaw moved to All Saints he adopted the 'English Use' here and writing in 1908 outlining his liturgical ambitions he expressed a desire to restore 'simplicity, unity, proportion, restraint and richness of colour' to a public worship that was 'fully English' and 'understanded of the people'. This was to be done within the confines of the *Book of Common Prayer*. Shaw partly achieved this goal by enhancing the setting of public worship. Medieval-inspired 'English' altars were installed, each adorned with riddel posts and a pair of candles. Shaw adopted English medieval vestments: albs, apparelled amices and full gothic chasubles. In the 1920s he would further enhance the church by erecting screens that enclosed the chancel and gave the interior a more authentic medieval feel.

Shaw was rector until 1956 and he continued to adapt the liturgy. In the later years of his incumbency, he shed his 'Prayer Book' catholic roots as he became increasingly drawn toward the Roman rite. A contemporary Roman Catholic veneer was added to communion, the number of altar candles increased and cassocks and Roman surplices (cottas), fiddle-back chasubles and rites such as Benediction of the Blessed Sacrament were introduced. This change of heart can partly be traced to the introduction of the newly published *English Missal* created after the Anglo-Catholic Congresses of the 1920s.

Today All Saints is a thriving inner city church catering for a congregation who come here to appreciate the liturgy that is offered. The liturgy is a mix of the English Use and the Roman rite and owes much to Shaw. Based around the English Missal, Solemn Mass on a Sunday evening is set to Merbecke's Common Prayer Noted and the plainsong setting Missa de Angelis with plainsong 'propers'. We mark the major feast days of the Christian year with a procession and Benediction.

LEFT: A procession on a feast day in Shaw's early years – from his book 'An Old York Church – All Hallows in North Street.'

North nave aisle

The tour of the church begins at the west end of the north nave aisle, close to the angle pier of the west tower. In the 1860s the remains of a medieval wall-painting of St Christopher could be seen on the north-east face of this pier. Fragments of pigment can still be discerned. The present **organ** was built in 1996 by Principal Pipe Organs of York.

Turn into the north aisle. The hexagonal **wooden pulpit** dates from 1675. Around the top is a text from St Paul's epistle to the Romans: 'And how shall they preach except they be sent', and on each side is a painted female figure, each representing a virtue, see Faith with a cross and Hope with an anchor.

Half way along the aisle, where there is a change in the form of roof, stood the medieval **altar to St Thomas the Martyr.** Over this, and reflecting in its iconography its location, is the **St Thomas window.** The left-hand lights portray the incredulity of St Thomas Apostle. We see the moment where doubting Thomas has plunged his hand into the Lord's wounded side, and at that moment recognises the risen Saviour: 'My Lord and my God'. To the right is a standing figure of an archbishop, vested in pallium and holding a cross staff. Despite the location of All Saints in York which had its own archbishop saint,

William, this is probably intended to be the more popular St Thomas of Canterbury, the dedicatee of the altar below – thereby completing the St Thomas imagery. This is probably the window which Reginald Bawtrie, a city merchant, left one hundred shillings to complete in 1429. The window originally included a kneeling image of Bawtrie and of his uncle, Sir John Bawtrie. These survive at the bottom of the next window, where Sir John (a member of the Minster clergy) is shown reading from a book inscribed with texts that invoke St Cecilia and St Lucy to pray for him.

TOP: *The head of Christ from the St Thomas window.*

LEFT: *Doubting Thomas about to plunge his hand into the side of the risen Christ.*

North choir aisle

Beyond the site of the altar of St Thomas, you enter the **choir of the Blessed Virgin Mary.** In the Middle Ages this contained an altar dedicated to our Lady and a statue of her with a light burning before it. In the Middle Ages the wealthier parishioners were accustomed to sit in this choir during mass and Nicholas Blackburn junior (see below) was buried beneath the seat he occupied here. The present altar of Our Lady is formed from the eighteenth-century communion table.

The western window in the chapel, the **Corporal Acts of Mercy window,** was formerly in the westernmost window opening of the north wall. It may have been given by, or erected as a memorial to Nicholas Blackburn senior (father of Nicholas junior) who was a merchant and mayor of York. Six of the seven corporal (bodily) acts of mercy are shown. These are from top to bottom and left to right: feeding the hungry, giving drink to the thirsty, offering hospitality to strangers, clothing the naked, visiting the sick and relieving those in prison. The final act of burying the dead is omitted. The bearded man, who in every panel is performing the 'works', is perhaps Nicholas Blackburn himself. The panels are set within fine contemporary canopywork, notice the angels who sit high up peering over the parapet.

TOP: *The interior of the Lady Chapel.*

LEFT: *The Corporal Acts of Mercy window.*

9

On the 14th day Death with his spear dramatically enters into the scene as all human life dies.

ABOVE: *The donors who paid for the Pricke of Conscience window look on in horror at the events portrayed above.*

BELOW: *The trees burn – a detail of the Pricke of Conscience window.*

RIGHT: *On the 11th day men and women come out and pray.*

The iconography of the next window is unique in European art. It is based on an anonymous Middle English poem called the **Pricke of Conscience**. The text of the *Pricke of Conscience* was concerned with the final fifteen days of the world. The window reads from bottom left to top right with each of the final days given a separate panel with a Middle English text that paraphrases the poem. The first nine panels are concerned with the physical destruction of the earth. This begins with the seas rising and falling and giving up monsters that *'make a roaring that is hideous to mans hearing.'* Then follows the destruction of buildings by an earthquake (see the new-built spire of All Saints falling), and the burning of all physical matter. The last panels illustrate the fate of frightened mankind, and the end of all things. Men hide in holes, emerging only to pray. Finally on the fourteenth day *'all that lives then shall die, both children, men and women.'* The end of things comes, the stars fall from the sky, the bones of the dead rise, and finally the *'the world burns on every side'*. As its name suggest the window is intended to be a moralistic call to repentance, so as a reminder of this, in the quatrefoil tracery lights at the top of the window, are two panels that show redeemed souls being let into heaven by St Peter and the dammed being taken to hell by demons. It is thought that members of the Henryson and Hessle families paid for this window. Both families, related by marriage, were among the freemen, who were the urban elite of medieval York. The kneeling figures of the families at the base of the window are particularly expressive and seem to look on in horror at the events going on in the panels above.

10

The mid-14th century glass in the **east window of the chapel** was formerly located in the east window of the chancel. It was moved and restored in the 1840s by Wailes of Newcastle. The iconography is that of the 'Joys of the Virgin', a summary of the major events in the Virgin Mary's life. The main panels at the bottom of the window are from left to right: the Annunciation, the Nativity, and Our Lord's Resurrection. The panels above portray the Adoration of the Magi, The Crucifixion and our Lady's Coronation as Queen of Heaven. The panels are set beneath elaborate canopies on a ground of trailing foliage, reminiscent of the glass produced by Robert Ketalbarn in the 1330s for the nave of York Minster.

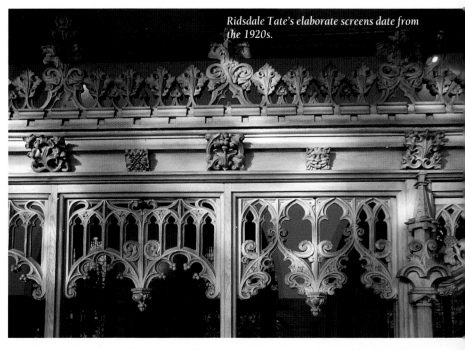

Ridsdale Tate's elaborate screens date from the 1920s.

The nativity – part of the Joys of the Virgin window of c1340.

In the niche in the wall to the south of the altar, is a fragment of an early 15th century statue, which until the early twentieth century was placed on a corbel set into the Pricke of Conscience window. This may represent a fragment of a **medieval statute of our Lady** and is contemporary with Emma Raughton (see above). Perhaps the particularly luxuriant hair was influenced by Emma Raughton's account of the Virgin Mary in her visions.

The parclose screens that divide the chancel from the chancel aisles, were designed by Edwin Ridsdale Tate (a former churchwarden) and date from the 1920s. Tate has incorporated a group of kneeling donors into the lower level of the western parclose.

If you walk through the door in the screen to the right of the Lady Chapel you enter the **Chancel.**

Chancel

The chancel ceiling, along with those that cover the chancel aisles, was erected during the incumbency of John Gilyot 1467-1472 and a boss over the altar bears his coat of arms. The hammerbeams of all three ceilings are in the form of angels who hold a variety of objects, including musical instruments and liturgical apparatus. One angel bears a soul (perhaps that of Gilyot) to heaven in a napkin. At the east-end of the chancel the paired angels are replaced with the Annunciation. Our Lady and Gabriel are opposite each other and he holds a scroll on which must have been painted his salute: 'Ave Maria, Gratia Plena' (Hail Mary, Full of Grace). The present colouring of the ceiling dates from 1977.

TOP: The roofs over the chancel and aisles were erected in the 1460s or 70s.

OTHERS: The hammerbeams of the ceiling are in the form of angels holding a variety of objects.

The stall that serves as the **sedilia** is also from Gilyot's time, and its misericord (tip-up seat) bears his coat of arms and initials, flanking a carving of the Pelican in her Piety, a symbol favoured by the Corpus Christi guild, of which Gilyot was master in 1472.

The stone **high altar** with its six candles dates from the later years of Patrick Shaw's incumbency. To the left of the altar, and slightly behind it, is a **double recess**, probably an aumbry for storing sacred vessels. To the right are the remains of the **blank arcade** that ran around the interior of the Early English chancel.

The glass in the east window behind the high altar, **The Blackburn window,** was originally positioned in the choir of our Lady where the Corporal Acts window is now located. The main figures are from left to right: St John the Baptist, St Ann teaching the Virgin to read and St Christopher. The figures are set under canopies with figures of prophets in the borders. A technique called backpainting, which involves painting details on two sides of the glass is used to good effect on the wimple of St Ann and the water surrounding the feet of St Christopher – giving a soft three-dimensional feel to the glass.

The imagery reflects the spiritual pre-occupations of the Blackburn family, who gave the window in the 1420s. The head of the family, Nicholas Blackburn senior (who also gave the Corporal Acts of Mercy window) had a particular fondness for St Ann and founded a chantry in the chapel of St Ann on Fossbridge, which he adorned with his best chalice and best vestment. In 1416 he gave £10 to Durham cathedral to erect a statue in the shrine of St Cuthbert, either to St Ann, St Christopher or St John the Baptist – precisely the same combination of saints that we see in this window. Nicholas senior and his son Nicholas junior (who is buried close by) and their respective wives (both called Margaret) are shown kneeling at the bottom of the window on either side of the Holy Trinity.

Nicholas senior is dressed in armour with a heraldic surcoat, an odd portrayal of a merchant that probably reflects his brief status as Admiral of the Northern Fleet in 1406-1407.

TOP: *The east window of the chancel was probably a memorial to Nicholas Blackburn senior, who died in 1432.*

LEFT: *The shield of arms of the Blackburn family in their window.*

South choir aisle

below. The most notable feature of the window are the six 14th-century roundels at the top of the lights and in the tracery. These are decorated with angels and drolleries, i.e. hybrid creatures, playing musical instruments.

The eastern window in the south wall, the **St Michael and St John window**, was reconstructed in 1965 from fragments scattered around the church. The two standing figures are of St Michael (left) and St John the Evangelist (right). Very little is left of the image of St Michael, who is shown in full plate armour slaying a blue dragon and weighing souls in a pair of scales. The figure of St John Evangelist, who is holding a palm and his eagle symbol, is better preserved. This window was probably paid for by James Baguley, a rector who died 1441 and four of his parishioners, including Robert Chapman and his wife. Sir James, the Chapmans and a further couple are kneeling at the base of the window.

Walk through the eastern set of screen doors from the sanctuary into the south aisle. As you do so, you enter an area of the church, which was known as the **choir of St Nicholas and St Katherine** in the Middle Ages. The altar, which is made of panels of 17th-century carving collected by Patrick Shaw, is dedicated to St Nicholas.

The **east window of the aisle (sII)** was heavily restored in 1844 and little medieval glass now remains. Of the 14th century are the figures of our Lady and St John that flank the cross, and the kneeling figures

ABOVE LEFT: The east window of the aisle was heavily restored by Wailes, but includes some 14th century glass.

ABOVE: The altar of St Nicholas incorporates 17th century woodwork collected by Patrick Shaw.

by an armoured angel who leads a group of priests. The figures that represent the *Virtues*, *Archangels* and *Angels*, are leading groups of average members of medieval York society. First are the middle-aged Burgesses, men like Nicholas Blackburn, who are accompanied by their wives in elaborate headresses. Working men and women are also shown: a labourer with a spade, a North Street tanner with his tools, a woman with a basket and a man holding up a pair of spectacles to his eyes. Perhaps they represent a group of parishioners who paid for the window.

LEFT: The angel representing Powers holds a Sun in Splendour banner.

RIGHT: The head of a lady – a detail from the Orders of Angels window.

BELOW: A detail of the Orders of Angels window – a man using a pair of medieval spectacles.

The next window was reconstructed from fragments in 1965 following the discovery of a 17th century drawing by Henry Johnston of the window in a complete state. The iconography is that of the **Nine Orders of Angels**. A representative angel of each order leads a procession of mortals of the appropriate rank in medieval society. From top left to bottom right: the figure representing the *Seraphim* leads a group of top-level clerics, a *Cherubim* leads a group of clerks and scholars, while the figure that represents the *Thrones* leads members of the medieval legal profession. The figure representing the *Dominations* leads a group including two kings, a pope and an emperor, that representing *Principalities* leads a group of noblemen, while *Powers* are represented

ABOVE: The 14th century grave slab of Thomas Collyngwyke – one of many medieval grave markers incorporated into the church floor.

ABOVE RIGHT: The interior of the choir of St Nicholas and St Katherine in the south aisle.

The south choir aisle also contains the most interesting monuments in the church (although more can be seen in the floor of the north aisle, and in the walls of the south porch and tower).

The first group can be found at the east end of the aisle. In the floor close to the screen is 15th century floriated cross bearing an inscription to Thomas and Juliana Collyngwyke, while beside it a slab of purbeck marble bears the indent of a lost brass to a priest. On the wall are two brass plates, the first in memory of Thomas Askwith, Sheriff of York (died 1609) and his wife, and the second in memory of Charles Towneley (died 1712) a Lancashire gentleman and friend of the diarist John Thoresby.

The second group are just beyond the 'Orders of Angels' window under the carpet on the aisle floor (which you are welcome to lift). Here is a brass in memory of Thomas Clerk, clerk to the city council (died 1482) and Margaret his wife, which includes in each corner a a symbol of one of the Evangelists. Intruded into the centre of the slab is a half-effigy of Thomas Atkinson, a tanner, who died in 1642. There is also a simple brass plate in memory of two Mayors of York, Robert Colynson (died 1458) and William Stokton (died 1471). They were successively the husbands of Isabella. Above on the wall is a monument to the architect John Etty. Etty 'who had acquired a great knowledge of Geometry and Architecture' was responsible for many of the large wooden altarpieces to be seen in York churches, was grandfather to the painter William and was also, apparently, a pupil of Grinling Gibbons.

South nave aisle

As you pass the last of these monuments you enter the south nave aisle. In the Middle Ages the east-end of the aisle contained the medieval altar of **St James the Great**.

Appropriately enough the first of the main figures in the next window (sVI) is St James, dressed in the garb of a pilgrim to his own shrine at Compestela. Next to him is our Lady crowned as Queen of Heaven and holding the Blessed Infant, and Christ appearing on the altar to an archbishop celebrating mass, perhaps St Martin or more likely St Gregory the Great. Robert Colynson (whose brass we have just seen in this aisle), asked in his will of 1450 for a priest

to sing a daily trental of St Gregory in the church for the space of three years, so perhaps he paid for the image of St Gregory in the window. The borders of the window incorporate angels playing instruments and the bottom panels contain fragments of lost glazing from other parts of the church. The major fragments include: the head of a bearded man in chainmail and helmet, two figures of prophets and a circular inscribed border to a heraldic device. There are also portions of canopies, inscriptions, heraldic devices and a merchant's mark.

If you turn around at this spot and look at the last set of hammerbeams in the south choir aisle roof, you will see that one of the angels is half scorched. This marks the extent of a fire that nearly destroyed the south nave aisle in 1997.

ABOVE: A miraculous mass – part of the window that stands over the site of the altar of St James.

LEFT: The bottom of the window contains late medieval glass fragments.

Move down the south nave aisle toward the font, as you do so you will pass over a number of medieval grave markers, including that of Sir John Bawtrie, the priest who is shown kneeling at the bottom of the Corporal Acts of Mercy window. Also notice the first pillar from the east, this is made from a Roman gritstone column, which was reused in the 12th-century church and again in a 15th century rebuild.

High up on the west wall of the aisle, above an old commandment board, can be seen a squint or opening, that probably allowed Emma Raughton a view of the altars in the church from her anchorhold. On the south-west angle pier of the tower is an early eighteenth century mace stand, which incorporates a list of some of the parishioners who have served as Lord Mayor of York.

Now move to the area of the **Nave** directly before the chancel screen. Like the parclose screens, the chancel screen and its rood group were erected in the 1920s to the design of Ridsdale Tate. To the north of the screen, and standing on a 14th-century corbel is an early 15th-century wooden statue of a sainted abbot: he is revered here as **St William of York.**

To the south of the screen, supported on a corbel by the sculptor Dick Reid, is the modern **shrine of our Lady of North Street.** The statue was erected in 1958 and is the focus of our devotion to Our

Lady. It is where our mass ends every Sunday evening with the *Angelus* and it is where this tour ends. As you stand before the image, you may wish to think of the men and women who built this church, who ministered here over the centuries, prayed in it, and were finally laid to rest beneath its roof. Perhaps you might offer a *Hail Mary,* an *Our Father* and a *Glory Be,* for them and for us all.

OPPOSITE PAGE: *The nave looking towards the chancel screen.*

LEFT: *The modern shrine of our Lady of North Street.*

The interior of the church from the south door.